DIVING AND SNORKELING GUIDE TO

Bonaire

Jerry Schnabel and Susan L. Swygert

Pisces Books™
A division of Gulf Publishing Company
Houston, Texas

Acknowledgments

The authors very much appreciate the assistance of Morey Ruza, Jack Chalk, and Captain Don Stewart of the Habitat; Laura Siegel of Photo Tours, NV; Andre and Gabrielle Nahr and Pam Teitel of Sand Dollar Dive and Photo; and Eric Newton of the Bonaire Marine Park.

All photos by Jerry Schnabel and Susan L. Swygert

This printing was revised by the authors and reprinted July 1996.

Library of Congress Cataloging-in-Publication Data

Schnabel, Jerry.
    Diving and snorkeling guide to Bonaire / Jerry Schnabel and Susan L. Swygert.
        p.   cm.
    ISBN 1-55992-043-2
    1. Skin diving — Bonaire — Guide-books. 2. Scuba diving — Bonaire — Guide-books. 3. Bonaire — Description and travel — Guide-books.
    I. Title.
GV840.S78S34   1991
797.2'3—dc20   90-47509
                                                        CIP

Publisher's note: At the time of publication of this book, all the information was determined to be as accurate as possible. However, new construction may have changed land reference points, weather may have altered reef configurations, and some businesses may no longer be in operation. Your assistance in keeping future editions up-to-date will be greatly appreciated.

Also, please pay particular attention to the diver rating system in this book. Know your limits!

Printed in Hong Kong

10   9   8   7   6   5   4

Table of Contents

*Dive sites suitable for snorkeling as well as for diving.

*Dive sites suitable for snorkeling as well as for diving.

Huge orange elephant ear sponges grow on wall slopes, making for excellent photo and video opportunities. Ebo's Reef, Klein Bonaire. (Photo: J. Schnabel) ▶

How to Use This Guide

Bonaire's unique coral reef system offers visiting divers many opportunities for diving from shore as well as from a boat. This guidebook describes the dive sites in detail. Use Chapter 2 , *Diving in Bonaire*, to find out if a particular dive site is consistent with your diving abilities, and also for information about currents, depths, entries, and points of interest. Bonaire is often referred to as the "Macro Capital of the Caribbean," and the auto license plates bear the words "Diver's Paradise." Read Chapter 3, *Marine Life of Bonaire*, to learn more about the tiny creatures that make up the unique macro world of Bonaire and about the many tropical fishes and corals. Chapter 4, *Safety,* will tell you some diving secrets of local island divemasters and instructors, which will help

Varieties of hard and soft corals, sea fans, and sponges make up Bonaire's fringing reef and provide shelter to the fish and invertebrate life living there. Boca Bartol, Washington Park. *(Photo: J. Schnabel)*

Elkhorn and mountainous star corals grow close to shore in the shallow water of the fringing reef. Boca Slagbaai, Washington Park. *(Photo: J. Schnabel)*

to make your dives safe and enjoyable. Additionally, information about the local chamber operation and DAN is provided for your easy reference.

Bonaire is equally fascinating abovewater, and is well known for its flamingos, parrots, and other bird life. Use Chapter 1, *Overview of Bonaire,* for topside activities, hotels, dining, shopping, and travel information. See Appendix 1 for a listing of dive operators and accommodations on Bonaire. This information will help you plan your trip.

The Rating System for Divers and Dives

Almost all shore dives in Bonaire begin in shallow water, from 10 to 20 feet deep, continuing to the edge of a typically sloping, sometimes vertical wall, which drops off to 130 feet or more, followed by a sand bottom that continues downward to infinite depths. Given this profile, any dive can be a shallow dive or a deep dive, with the exception of a dive off a boat moored in deeper water. For this reason, *typical depth range* will indicate the depth range you will encounter at each site, from the average depth on top of the reef to a depth where the reef ends and the sandy slope begins. It should be kept in mind that the safe limit for

The Christmas tree worm (Spirobranchus gigantus) *extends colorful fan-like apparatus to filter-feed on small planktonic organisms passing through the water column. (Photo: S. Swygert)*

sport diving is 130 feet and this guide does not recommend exceeding this limit.

We consider a *novice* diver to be someone in decent physical condition, who has recently completed a SCUBA diving certification course, or a certified diver who has not been diving recently or has no experience in similar waters. We consider an *intermediate* diver to be a certified diver in excellent physical condition who has been diving actively for at least one year following certification, and who has been diving recently in similar waters. We consider an *advanced* diver to be someone who has completed an advanced SCUBA diving certification course, has been diving recently in similar waters, and is in excellent physical condition. Because one can arrive in Bonaire and go diving without an instructor or divemaster, and given the reef profile of deep water close to shore, it is recommended that novice divers make their first dive in Bonaire with an instructor or local guide. Current conditions are listed as *light, moderate,* and *heavy.* Obviously currents, waves, and weather can vary at times and you need to assess your abilities honestly. A good rule to follow is that if there is any apprehension at all about a certain dive, don't make it! Rather, move on to something you feel more comfortable with.

1

Overview of Bonaire

Bonaire is definitely equipped to handle diving and divers. More than 19,000 divers visit Bonaire yearly. The facilities available have expanded and include everything from live-aboard dive boats to lovely inns, villas, and splendid hotels. The local people are extremely friendly and eager to help. The hospitable nature of Bonaireans is attributable to their security about Bonaire, and the stability of the Dutch influence there.

Originally discovered in 1499 by the Spanish on an expedition led by Alonso de Ojeda and Amerigo Vespucci, the island was first named Isla de Brasil or Island of Dyewood. Native Caiquetio and Arawak Indians inhabited the island at the time of its discovery. They were described by the Spanish as living in the stone age, with mud huts for houses. The dye from the Dyewood tree was used by the Indians as a medium of expression in their cave paintings, which can still be visited today at Boca Onima and other locations. As a part of the Spanish colonization of the island, they removed the Indian population and enslaved them in the copper mines of Hispaniola in 1515. Traces of the Indian population can be seen physically in only a few of today's Bonaireans.

The Dutch acquired Curaçao in 1634, a much-needed naval base in their war against Spain. In 1636, Bonaire and neighboring Aruba fell to the Dutch and Bonaire became a colony of the Netherlands. The Dutch West India Company began to produce salt in 1639, and today salt production is integral to Bonaire's economy. Between 1800 and 1816, the Dutch were plagued by British and French privateers and did not fully recover control of the island's development until this period was over.

In 1954, Bonaire and the other islands of the Netherlands Antilles became autonomous from Holland, at which time funds were granted for development of various resources. On January 1, 1986, Bonaire became a territory of the Kingdom of the Netherlands, now consisting of three major territories: the Netherlands (Holland), the Netherlands Antilles (Bonaire, Curaçao, Saba, St. Eustatius, and St. Maarten), and Aruba. This leaves the development of tourism and other resources to the Netherlands Antilles, with matters of defense and foreign affairs being the

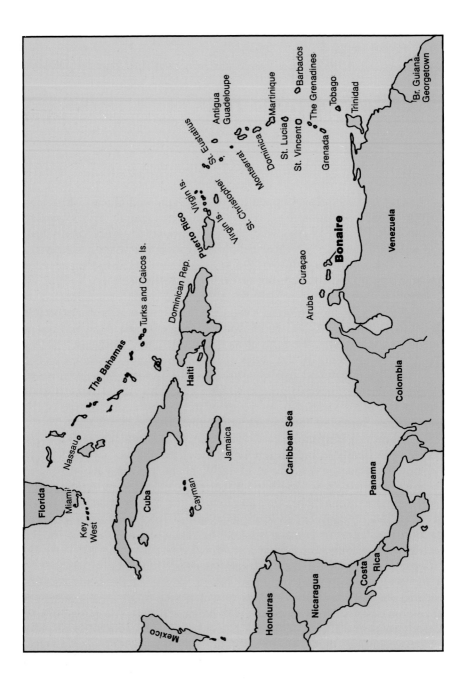

Florida
Key West
Miami

Mexico
Honduras
Nicaragua
Costa Rica
Panama
Colombia

Cuba
Cayman
Jamaica
Nassau
The Bahamas
Turks and Caicos Is.
Haiti
Dominican Rep.
Puerto Rico
Virgin Is.

Caribbean Sea

Aruba
Curaçao
Bonaire
Venezuela

St. Christopher
St. Eustatius
Montserrat
Antigua
Guadeloupe
Dominica
Martinique
St. Lucia
St. Vincent
Barbados
The Grenadines
Grenada
Tobago
Trinidad

Br. Guiana
Georgetown

Dense coral growth close to shore makes Bonaire an excellent snorkeling and diving destination. Wayaca, Washington Park. (Photo: J. Schnabel)

responsibility of the Kingdom of the Netherlands. This system has made it possible for Bonaire to enter the 21st century and develop at its own chosen pace.

Bonaire Today

Bonaire can best be described as an arid, mountainous island with desert vegetation and an ironshore coastline surrounded by clear turquoise waters, abundant with magnificent coral formations. Bonaire is about 24 miles long and 3–7 miles wide, and is located just 50 miles north of Venezuela and 30 miles east of Curaçao. West of Bonaire is the tiny island of Klein Bonaire, a 1,500 acre circular island with a fringing reef, where some of Bonaire's best dive sites lie. Klein Bonaire is uninhabited and bordered by several beaches and coves. Bonaire has a population of 11,500 native Antilleans, representing a mix of Dutch, Spanish, and Indian cultures.

Kralendijk, the capital city of Bonaire, is both quaint and picturesque. Dutch architecture is colorful and bold, providing this seaside town with its own unique atmosphere. Southern Bonaire is flat and home of the Antillean International Salt Company, where evaporation pools produce incredible salt deposits. These deposits are scraped up by heavy bulldozers and loaded onto ships by way of conveyer belts at the rate of 2,000 tons per hour. Salt is exported to the United States, the Caribbean, and New Zealand. Modern Bonaire is a mix of light industry and tourism. By far the greatest employer on Bonaire is the tourist industry.

The 13,500 acre Washington/Slagbaai National Park makes up much of northern Bonaire. The park is a wildlife preserve and is the first of its kind in the Netherlands Antilles. There is no camping, hunting, or fishing allowed, and visitors cannot interfere with the normal behavior of the one-hundred-plus species of birds and flamingos found there. The park is also home to native iguanas, and goats roam freely through the mountains. Mt. Brandaris, at 784 feet, has the highest elevation in Bonaire and is located in the park. Diving is allowed in the park, with many excellent locations. The tiny village of Rincon, which lies just outside of the park, is the oldest settlement in Bonaire. Nestled in among the mountains, the people of Rincon are some of the most friendly on Bonaire.

One of the best surprises about Bonaire is the weather. It's almost always sunny, with an average rainfall of only 22 inches per year. The

Colorful Dutch architecture is characteristic of the many government and commercial buildings in Bonaire. Kralendijk. (Photo: S. Swygert)

temperature averages a pleasant 82 degrees. Located below the hurricane belt, Bonarie is a good destination for divers year-round. English is spoken by most of the native population, although Papiamento and Dutch are the native languages. Spanish is also spoken and understood, but used to a lesser degree than the other languages.

Hotels and Accommodations

Bonaire is the home of full-service dive hotels, offering everything from fine dining and lovely rooms to streamlined dive operations, photo centers, tennis courts, casinos, shops, and swimming pools. There are four hotels and one condominium development on Bonaire offering these amenities. Another hotel and condominium project is under development. One hotel already has timeshare apartments, and another timeshare project is planned. The major hotels are located close to the town of Kralendijk, and most within walking distance of the downtown shops. Other accommodations include various inns, guesthouses, private villas, and apartments, all of which are of recent, modern construction offering high standards of accommodations, with bedrooms, kitchens, and living rooms, as well as pools and beaches. Dive packages are available at both the hotels and at other types of accommodations.

Lovely Spanish-style villas accent modern Bonaire's leeward coastline. Captain Don's Habitat. *(Photo: J. Schnabel)*

A blazing sunset enhances this seaside dining experience. Bonaire has an excellent assortment of restaurants to choose from. Chibi-chibi Restaurant. *(Photo: J. Schnabel)*

Dining, Shopping, and Sightseeing

Most hotels have excellent restaurants. However, there are many good restaurants in downtown Kralendijk. Fresh seafood is a favorite among many tourists, with specialties such as Indonesian, Chinese, pasta, and native dishes also available. Fast food chains have not yet arrived on Bonaire. There is one local pizza shop, an ice cream parlor, and several native sandwich shops located within walking distance of most accommodations. The local tourist newspaper, *Bonaire Holiday,* lists the restaurants, buffets, and eateries on Bonaire. Dress is usually casual; however, some restaurants are encouraging more upscale attire.

Kralendijk features many new shops, and there is even a new shopping mall. Everything is available, from fine jewelry to cameras, electronic equipment, perfumes, books, liquors, leathers, imported gift items from Europe, clothing, and South American crafts. Many of the hotels have gift shops and boutiques carrying a variety of tropical beachwear, gifts, and clothing. The downtown area has undergone a major face-lift, which reflects the Dutch architectural style. The famous town pier usually has one or two tugboats tied alongside, adding a certain charm to the waterfront area. Many of the restaurants are located seaside, giving a nice view of passing sailboats and colorful sunsets. Guided sightseeing tours are available through tour operators, and one shop even has guided bird-watching expeditions.

Transportation

Travel to Bonaire usually requires you to fly via ALM Antillean Airlines. There are daily flights to Bonaire thru Curaçao, and direct flights on weekends from New York and Miami. Many different airlines offer daily flights to Aruba and Curaçao, which connect with ALM Antillean Airlines or Air Aruba to Bonaire.

Once on Bonaire, you will find rental cars readily available through Budget, Avis, Dollar, and other sources. Taxi service is available from the airport to your hotel, and also to shops and restaurants. As beach diving is so popular on Bonaire, many new jeeps and four-wheel-drive vehicles are available for rent. During the peak tourist seasons, it is a very good idea to reserve your vehicle in advance. Some hotels and guest houses rent motor bikes and have bicycles available. There is a U.S. $10 departure tax at the airport when leaving on an international flight.

Direct jet flights to Bonaire are available via ALM Antillean Airlines. The airport has been recently reconstructed to accommodate more tourist traffic. (Photo: J. Schnabel)

Customs and Immigration

Upon entering Bonaire, you will be asked to produce a return ticket, proof of citizenship, and an immigration form, which is given out during your flight. Usually a passport is preferred, although a voter's registration card or birth certificate is also acceptable. Local customs agents are required to search incoming bags. Any spear guns will be removed, as spearfishing is illegal in Bonaire. Should you be traveling with excessive photographic equipment (say, more than five cases), you may be asked to register the equipment with customs and post a bond equal to the import duty of the equipment. This is then redeemable when the equipment leaves the island. For any major commercial film projects, it is advisable to work through the Bonaire Tourist Bureau to avoid these problems. If you are returning to the U.S., any film, paintings, works of art, antiques, foreign language books, or sculptures are duty-free items. You will also be allowed to bring duty free up to U.S. $400 worth of articles, one carton of cigarettes, and one quart of liquor.

Friendly Bonaireans will be glad to show you how to enjoy the latest watersports equipment available at many hotels.
Sunset Beach Hotel.
(Photo: J. Schnabel)

The Maduro & Curiel's Bank building — a strong banking community underlies the island's development. (Photo: J. Schnabel)

Foreign Exchange

The Netherlands Antilles guilder or florin (NAf.) is a sound currency backed by gold and foreign exchange. The U.S. dollar buys 1.77 guilders; both dollars and guilders are used on Bonaire. Should you be passing through Aruba, remember that the Aruba guilder is not acceptable in Bonaire, and the Bonairean guilder is not acceptable in Aruba. This is a result of Aruba's recent independence from the Netherlands Antilles. Change at local stores will usually be given in NAf., and some merchants use 1.75 NAf. to the dollar. Hotels will usually give change in U.S. dollars. Should you need to convert a large sum of money, it is best to go to the local banks even though there will be a small charge for the conversion.

Diving in Bonaire

Water conditions are ideal for all levels of divers and snorkelers, and Bonaire's beautiful reefs and marine life are truly paradise for the underwater photographer, beginning or advanced. There are endless opportunities and the photo/video facilities are among the best to be found on any island.

Bonaire's north/south alignment protects the entire western coastline from the force of wind and waves generated by the prevailing eastern trade winds (see the map on p. 22). Also to the leeward is Klein Bonaire, an uninhabited island one mile west of Bonaire, and the coasts of both islands are bordered with lush, healthy coral reefs just perfect for snorkeling and SCUBA diving.

Bonaire's underwater topography is distinctive as the drop-off to deep water is very close to shore. Large branching elkhorn and staghorn corals dot the shallow terrace close to shore and near the reef's crest, giant soft coral gorgonians, brain coral, and mountainous star coral colonies form a dense habitat that nurtures and shelters many species of fish and invertebrates. The gently sloping drop-off is studded with massive colorful sponges and cascading hard coral colonies. There are also several artificial reefs, like piers and wrecks, to dive and explore.

The fingerprint snail (Cyphoma signatum) *is very uncommon, and is almost always found on fans and soft corals, upon which it feeds.* Leonora's Reef, Klein Bonaire. *(Photo: S. Swygert)*

Bonaire Marine Park

The park was founded in 1979 to preserve and protect Bonaire's natural beauty and marine resources. An annual user fee of US $10.00 is charged for admission and a colorful personal marine park tag that must be easily visible to park rangers.

Bonaire has a long history of reef conservation. In 1962, Captain Don Stewart, Bonaire's respected diving pioneer, placed his first permanent mooring, enabling a boat to visit a dive site without using an anchor. During these early years, all the dive operators teamed up to place additional moorings at many spectacular sites, and the use of spearguns was outlawed. By 1979, a grant from the World Wildlife Fund made it possible to legally create the Bonaire Marine Park with the understanding that the park must be self-sufficient within three years. Private donations were helpful in supplementing funds for projects, such as the 1987 Sea Tether Project, developed by Captain Don and aimed at creating 100 moored dive sites. In 1991, an admission fee was established to provide a continuous source of funding for the Bonaire Marine Park. The program is enthusiastically supported by residents and visitors, and the park's staff has been able to maintain the moorings, provide bright yellow shore dive markers, produce brochures and dive maps for each resort, and develop many educational and research programs, such as introducing the local children to the sea through a learn-to-snorkel program and monitoring the recent Caribbean phenomenon of coral bleaching.

Serving as a model for other islands, Bonaire was first in the Caribbean to protect the entire coral reef ecosystem in all waters surrounding Bonaire and Klein Bonaire from the high-water line to a depth of 200 feet. All dive operators encourage divers to practice diving techniques consistent with reef protection and free buoyancy control workshops are offered.

Bonaire Marine Park Rules
- You must have a valid admission ticket to the marine park.
- Anchoring is forbidden.
- Spearfishing and spearguns are forbidden.
- It is forbidden to remove anything living or dead from the Park (with the exception of garbage!).
- Do not damage the reefs; avoid touching the coral and silting up the bottom.

The reef begins just a few feet from shore, and the clear and warm water invites snorkelers. Fish feeding is a favorite activity. Calabas. *(Photo: J. Schnabel)*

Dive Sites

The dive sites discussed are installed and maintained by the Council of Underwater Resort Operators of Bonaire (CURO). These dive sites are moored with buoys from Sea Tether and the Aggressor Fleet Ltd. and are placed for access by dive boats. With the exception of the Klein Bonaire sites, most sites are accessible from shore. We shall discuss 40 sites, which are divided geographically as South, Klein Bonaire, North, and Washington Park. These sites include many new moorings and are selected to give you a cross section of what to expect from each region. Sites that are temporarily closed are not discussed.

There are currently 63 moored sites in Bonaire and Klein Bonaire. There are 19 additional sites that await mooring lines or have been temporarily closed (Twixt, Valerie's Hill, Mi Dushi, Ebo's Special, Knife, and Petrie's Pillar). Another 8 sites await placement of moorings. This totals 90 moored sites expected to be in place by late 1991. In addition to these sites, there are an infinite number of shore diving possibilities for those who wish to explore the island's extensive lee coastline. The symbol * beside a site name will indicate that this site is also recommended for snorkelers.

The banded coral shrimp (Stenopus hispidus) *is a distinctive member of the reef community. It waves its long white antennae to attract fish for cleaning.* Southwest Corner, Klein Bonaire. *(Photo: S. Swygert)*

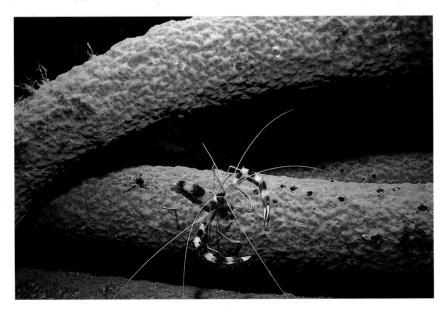

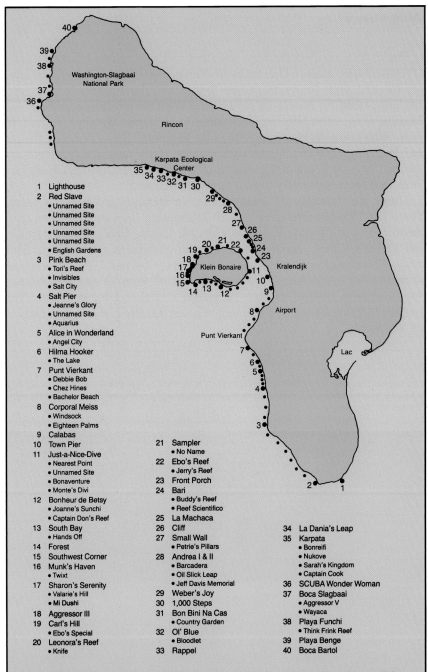

40

39

38

Washington-Slagbaai
National Park

37

36

Rincon

Karpata Ecological
Center

35 34 33 32 31 30

29

28

27

26

25

24

23

20 21 22

19

18

17   Klein Bonaire   11

16

15   14 13 12   10

9

Kralendijk

8   Airport

Punt Vierkant

7

6

5

4

3

Lac

2   1

1   Lighthouse
2   Red Slave
    • Unnamed Site
    • Unnamed Site
    • Unnamed Site
    • Unnamed Site
    • Unnamed Site
    • English Gardens
3   Pink Beach
    • Tori's Reef
    • Invisibles
    • Salt City
4   Salt Pier
    • Jeanne's Glory
    • Unnamed Site
    • Aquarius
5   Alice in Wonderland
    • Angel City
6   Hilma Hooker
    • The Lake
7   Punt Vierkant
    • Debbie Bob
    • Chez Hines
    • Bachelor Beach
8   Corporal Meiss
    • Windsock
    • Eighteen Palms
9   Calabas
10   Town Pier
11   Just-a-Nice-Dive
    • Nearest Point
    • Unnamed Site
    • Bonaventure
    • Monte's Divi
12   Bonheur de Betsy
    • Joanne's Sunchi
    • Captain Don's Reef
13   South Bay
    • Hands Off
14   Forest
15   Southwest Corner
16   Munk's Haven
    • Twixt
17   Sharon's Serenity
    • Valarie's Hill
    • Mi Dushi
18   Aggressor III
19   Carl's Hill
    • Ebo's Special
20   Leonora's Reef
    • Knife

21   Sampler
    • No Name
22   Ebo's Reef
    • Jerry's Reef
23   Front Porch
24   Bari
    • Buddy's Reef
    • Reef Scientifico
25   La Machaca
26   Cliff
27   Small Wall
    • Petrie's Pillars
28   Andrea I & II
    • Barcadera
    • Oil Slick Leap
    • Jeff Davis Memorial
29   Weber's Joy
30   1,000 Steps
31   Bon Bini Na Cas
    • Country Garden
32   Ol' Blue
    • Bloodlet
33   Rappel

34   La Dania's Leap
35   Karpata
    • Bonreifi
    • Nukove
    • Sarah's Kingdom
    • Captain Cook
36   SCUBA Wonder Woman
37   Boca Slagbaai
    • Aggressor V
    • Wayaca
38   Playa Funchi
    • Think Frink Reef
39   Playa Benge
40   Boca Bartol

Note: Only numbered dive sites are discussed. Indented sites are marked on the map by small dots between the numbered sites to which they are similar.

South

Lighthouse 1

Typical depth range   : 20–80 feet
Typical current conditions : Moderate to heavy
Expertise required   : Advanced
Access   : Shore

This site has no permanent mooring buoy as it can seldom be dived due to heavy waves and surge. However, the Willemstoren lighthouse marks the southernmost point of the island and is an excellent dive when the weather is calm. Dive booties will be a necessity. As with most of Bonaire's shore entries, you will have to walk over some rocks and stones to enter the water. Begin your dive into the current and return to your exit point with the assistance of the current. As current conditions change,

The gently swaying sea fans always grow parallel to the shore in shallow water. The netlike branches spread across the surge path, and the polyps feed on plankton. Lighthouse Reef. *(Photo: J. Schnabel)*

Silvery schools of horse-eye jacks (Caranx latus) *rove the open ocean, but often swim along the reef in search of small baitfish. (Photo: J. Schnabel)*

you will have to determine which direction the current is running and swim against it.

This site is characterized by large sea fans in the shallows, and heavy soft and hard coral growth as you approach the drop-off. The wall face slopes down quickly to 80 feet before sloping off to sand. There are many trumpetfish in the shallows, along with schoolmasters, margates, and turtles. In the deeper water, you can often encounter tarpons cruising eastward, and in the open blue water it's not uncommon to see large schools of jacks and cubera snappers. Lighthouse also has large tiger groupers along the wall face. If waves are crashing onshore and there is any white water at all, it is not advisable to dive this site. Only dive here when it is very calm. Just a few hundred yards to the east of the lighthouse lie the remains of a freighter that went aground there.

Red Slave 2

Typical depth range	: 20–80 feet
Typical current conditions	: Moderate to heavy
Expertise required	: Advanced
Access	: Shore

Red Slave refers to the second set of slave huts on the road south from Kralendijk. If you go too far, you will be at the lighthouse. You can enter the water just in front of the slave huts. The current here is usually a factor, running from north to south. Begin diving into the current swimming north, and return with the current going south to your exit point. The danger in drift diving here from shore is that there is no way to tell when you have rounded the corner and are drifting east into heavy seas for a difficult surf exit. For this reason, drift diving at Red Slave is only safe from boats.

There is a prolific growth of soft corals, sea fans, and sponges along the drop-off is in the shallows at 15–25 feet deep. Only 60 feet from shore intermittent sand shoots plunge over the wall slope to a depth of 100 feet, where the reef ends and the sand bottom begins. Schools of horse-eye jacks, snappers, and often porpoises can be seen or heard. Turtles are also quite common to this site.

The long, slender body and typically reddish-brown coloring of the trumpetfish (Aulostomus maculatus) *enables an effective camouflage amongst soft corals. Normal color changes include bright yellow to bright blue. (Photo: J. Schnabel)*

Typical depth range	:	25–90 feet
Typical current conditions	:	Light to moderate
Expertise required	:	Intermediate
Access	:	Shore or boat

Pink Beach is the long sand beach just north of the northernmost slave huts. Enter the water by the parking area at the abandoned building that marks the beginning of the beach. A dive buoy is located offshore of this site. Begin your dive by swimming into the current. Snorkeling is good anywhere off the beach, and the beach makes a good place for an all-day outing. The shallows here have a longer swim to the drop-off. It's about 100 yards across a sandy flat with numerous soft corals and primarily staghorn coral formations to reach the reef crest.

The delightful lined seahorse (Hippocampus erectus) *is truly one of the signatures of Bonaire and, although common, are hard to find as they blend in so well with their habitat. (Photo: S. Swygert)*

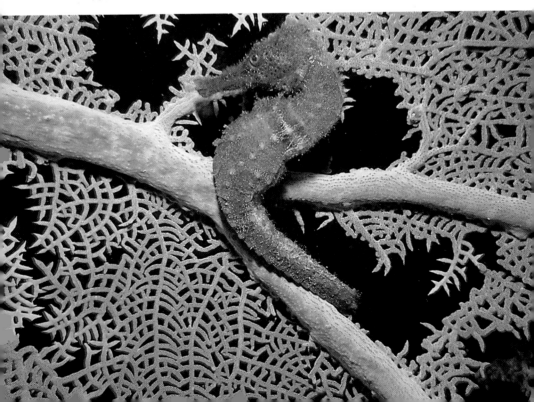

The protected hawksbill turtle (Eretmochelys imbricata) *can be seen soaring along any of the reefs of Bonaire. Remember that turtles are reptiles and thus air breathers. (Photo: J. Schnabel)*

The crest of the slope, at 30–40 feet deep, is densely populated by pristine corals. The wall face has many purple and iridescent vase sponges. Frogfish can occasionally be found along the reef shoulder, along with scorpionfish, peacock flounders, stingrays, schools of goatfish, and an occasional turtle. Schools of horse-eye jacks often swim through in about 80 feet of water. The macro life here is also good, with numerous anemones and arrow crabs; sometimes even seahorses may be spotted among the lush gorgonians covering the sloping drop-off.

Salt Pier 4

Typical depth range	:	15–50 feet
Typical current conditions	:	Light
Expertise required	:	Novice to intermediate
Access	:	Shore

This dive site is one of the best for the photographer, either with a macro or wide-angle lens. The opportunities are endless. This site also makes an exceptional night dive. Park just under the Salt Company's overhead conveyer belt close to shore. Entry is easy over some large flat concrete blocks or at the small rocky beach. Swim out under the pilings for 80 yards, to the spot where the pilings form a T-shape, with one set going north and the other set going south. Please bear in mind that this is a working pier. Do not dive here if a ship is approaching the Salt Pier or or when a vessel is docked.

The pilings are covered with incredible sponge and coral growth. Soft coral bushes are prolific on the pilings, as is orange tubastrea coral, which puts on a splendid display at night. The pilings begin on the coastal side in just 20 feet of water and reach to 50 feet on the drop-off side as the reef slope drops off to deeper water. There is no need to go any deeper than 50 feet, as there is more to see on and around the pier. Whether you travel north or south along the pilings, you won't be disappointed. There are schools of goatfish and creole wrasses under the pilings, with many tiger groupers cruising through.

French angelfish and queen angelfish are in abundance here, and some pilings have the juveniles of each swimming close to protected areas. Schools of surgeonfish and blue tangs clean the pilings of algae. Macro life is excellent — tiny crabs, shrimps, and fish inhabit the thick growths on the pilings.

Piers and wrecks can form a basis for an artificial reef. The Salt Pier pilings are densely covered with an amazing variety of colorful sponges and corals, and many invertebrates shelter amongst the growth. (Photo: J. Schnabel) ▶

Typical depth range	:	30–100 feet
Typical current conditions	:	Light
Expertise required	:	Intermediate
Access	:	Shore or boat

   The dive buoy is located just south of the Trans World Radio towers, and marks the entry point from shore. This site is on the southern end of a double-reef system, which runs parallel to shore and follows north to Pt. Vierkant. This site is characterized by a flat reef in the shallow zone with staghorn coral, finger coral, and lots of soft coral gorgonians. This continues out to 35–40 feet deep where the slope downward begins. This slope ends in a sand valley anywhere from 80–100 feet deep. It's a short swim of 60 feet across the sand to the second reef, which has

The southern reefs of Bonaire feature a double-reef system. Offshore, the reef slopes down to a sand channel at approx. 60–100', and a second reef reaches up to 40–50' and then drops off steeply. (Photo: J. Schnabel)

The black margate (Anisotremus surinamensis) *is a large and shy member of the grunt family. Normally solitary, it hovers just off the reef in the shelter of soft corals or large sponges. (Photo: J. Schnabel)*

large formations of boulder coral, mountainous star coral, and brain corals. The second or outer reef rises up from the sand to 50 feet deep in some places and then proceeds to drop off to very deep water.

The shallow-water fish life is populated with French angelfish, parrot-fishes, rock beauties, and banded butterflyfish. This site is also home to an occasional green moray eel. Throughout the double reef system, white-spotted and scrawled filefish are regularly seen. The sand flats host sting-rays and garden eels, while the outer reef is home to large schools of black margates and schoolmaster snappers.

Typical depth range	:	60–100 feet
Typical current conditions	:	Light
Expertise required	:	Advanced
Access	:	Shore or boat

Urgently needing repairs, the *Hilma Hooker* docked at Bonaire's Town Pier, but suspicious customs officers discovered a cargo of marijuana. Police burned the cargo, and the dive operators of Bonaire decided to sink the vessel in the sand between the unique double-reef system in the Angel City area. In 1984, the sea valves were opened and the *Hooker* became a permanent dive site. A cluster of dive buoys marks the site just in front of the Trans World Radio towers.

The *Hooker* is a 235-foot-long steel-hulled freighter, which rests on her starboard side in 100 feet of water. The vessel's stern lies to the north and the bow to the south. None of the hatches and entrances have been sealed and it is still possible to penetrate the wreck. Divers are requested to only explore the outer areas of the wreck and the large cargo holds. **Do not enter areas where you cannot see light marking a clear exit path.** It is dangerous to penetrate wrecks without proper training, especially wrecks with hatches and doors that appear to be in working order. Hinges may work to allow entrance, but may be impossible to reopen to exit. The top of the wreck is just 60 feet deep, and the stern section has good coral growth around the propeller and ship's wheel. The central section has large open cargo holds, through which you can safely explore interior sections of the wreck. The bow section has a large mast that reaches to the outer reef, with the crow's nest still intact.

Barracuda, schools of French grunts, mahogany snappers, and large groupers have made this dive site their home. There are abundant yellowtail snappers and some friendly French angelfish. The reef system extending from shore drops down from 30 feet deep, ending in sand at 100 feet deep. The wreck lies up against the first reef, running in a north to south direction parallel to shore. You must swim about 30 yards to cross the sand valley to the outer reef, which rises up to 80 feet deep and then drops down on the outside to depths in excess of 130 feet. The best way to dive the Hooker is to first explore the stern section, working your way down the wreck, and then to double back to the first reef and ascend onto the shallow reef to finish your dive in 30 feet of water.

The Hilma Hooker *wreck is an intact freighter off the southern coast, resting at a maximum depth of 100'. Sunk in 1984, this artificial reef now shelters small schools of grunts. This steering wheel is located at the stern. (Photo: S. Swygert)* ▶

Typical depth range	: 30–100 feet
Typical current conditions	: Light
Expertise required	: Novice
Access	: Shore or boat

To get to this dive site, follow the road south to a small lighthouse. The first dive buoy south of this lighthouse marks the dive site, which is north of the Trans World Radio towers. There is now a condominium project under construction there, aptly named Lighthouse Beach Resort. The shallow zone of this site is a mix of staghorn corals, finger corals, and gorgonians. Mountainous star coral, brain coral, sponges, and soft corals decorate the reef slope down to the sand channel in 70–100 feet of water. The outer reef is low in profile, with schoolmasters, groupers, and bar jacks swimming among the corals.

Towards the southern portion of the reef, there is a coral structure that connects the outer reef with the inner reef. This is a good point to turn back to the shallow reef and explore the inner reef face. As with all of the double reef sites, the outer drop-off wall is not worth exploring due to its depth. There are numerous yellowtail snappers that will accompany you on your dive looking for a handout. Scrawled filefish, Spanish hogfish, and rock beauties add brilliant color to the upper reef slope. Barracudas often frequent this area.

Rarely found schooling in Bonaire, the barracuda (Sphyraena barracuda) *enjoys cleaning stations. Undeserving of its fierce reputation, the shy barracuda always yields to a diver's approach. (Photo: S. Swygert)*

Corporal Meiss 8

Typical depth range	:	30–100 feet
Typical current conditions	:	Light
Expertise required	:	Novice
Access	:	Shore or boat

This new site, located between Lighthouse Point and Windsock, has been added to the CURO list since 1989. The shallow reef here consists of elkhorn coral very close to shore, with staghorn coral, soft corals, and isolated coral heads extending out to 30 feet of water. The reef slope is gradual, beginning in 30 feet and descending to 100 feet, where a sand bottom begins and is broken up by scattered coral clusters and gorgonians. The upper reef slope is primarily mountainous star coral, gorgonians, and numerous purple tube sponges and large orange sponges.

Sponges are the most primitive of multicelled animals, yet by serving as filters, they are vital to the ecology of the reef. The colorful giant tube sponge (Aplysina lacunosa) *is abundant at most of Bonaire's dive sites. (Photo: J. Schnabel)*

The intermediate spotted drum (Equetus punctatus) *is a bottom-dwelling fish noted for its unusually tall front dorsal fin. As it matures, the short dorsal fin and tail will be fully spotted. (Photo: J. Schnabel)*

Mahogany snappers are plentiful, goldentail morays emerge from crevices in the coral, and trumpetfish interact with the soft corals. Schoolmasters, French angelfish, queen angelfish, and rock beauties are present on the upper slopes. Tiger groupers, squirrelfish, blackbar soldierfish, and spotted drums are associated with corals of the sloping wall face. This new site is both good for wide-angle and macro photography. Sea anemones and small sponge formations provide good invertebrate habitats.

Typical depth range	: 20–90 feet
Typical current conditions	: Light
Expertise required	: Novice
Access	: Shore

This reef runs parallel to shore in front of the Flamingo Beach Resort and the Carib Inn. It is good for snorkelers and photographers, as well as for training dives. You can enter from any one of the Dive Bonaire piers or the Carib Inn dock. The shallow area has some staghorn coral and isolated coral heads. There are lots of fish to see in this area. French angelfish, both adults and juveniles, parrotfish of all varieties, and Spanish hogfish are common. In the shallow water, there is abundant invertebrate life with many anemones and small sponge formations.

The reef crest is at about 30 feet deep and slopes down to 90 feet, where it levels out into sand. The wall slope is good for wide-angle photography, as there are purple tube sponges, orange sponges, and nice formations of mountainous star coral along the upper edge of the slope. Just in front of the Calabas restaurant pier, in 25 feet of water, is a large anchor, and below this, in 50–80 feet of water, lies an aluminum lifeboat that is well-encrusted with coral and sponge growth, making it a good subject for underwater photography. This site is also a good night dive for both snorkelers and divers.

Throughout the reefs of Bonaire, old anchors are found. Thoroughly encrusted with corals and sponges, they are great indicators of Bonaire's history, as well as superb photo subjects. (Photo: J. Schnabel)

Typical depth range	: 15–40 feet
Typical current conditions	: Light
Expertise required	: Novice
Access	: Shore

Located next to the customs office, there are usually one or two tugboats tied alongside the pier. It is customary to check with the harbormaster to see if there are any ships expected that could pose a danger to divers below. The pier has recently undergone a major reconstruction project, and many of the coral-encrusted pilings were rebuilt, much to the dismay of local divers. However, the pier is still an excellent dive site, and one especially good for the underwater photographer.

The pilings stretch out away from shore about 350 feet and then extend north for another 250 feet. The average depth below the pier is 20 feet, and on the outside edge it reaches depths of 40 feet. It's always a good idea to stay down along the bottom and directly beneath the pier in an area where there is boat traffic. The pilings are covered with prolific

No dive vacation to Bonaire could be complete without a night dive at the famous Town Pier. The flowerlike polyps of the tube corals are extended for nighttime feeding and resemble vivid yellow bouquets. (Photo: S. Swygert)

The pilings of the Town Pier are encrusted with orange tube coral (Tubastrea coccinea). *This coral can grow well only in shaded areas, which is why the pier fosters such a prolific display of this colorful coral. (Photo: J. Schnabel)*

growths of purple and yellow tube sponges, orange tubastrea corals, gorgonians, and red fire sponge.

Macro life is abundant on the pilings. Small crabs, seahorses, frogfish, arrowhead crabs, and banded coral shrimps can all be found here, just to name a few. Sheltering under the pier are schools of French grunts, squirrelfish, French angelfish, trumpetfish, and rock beauties. At night the orange tubastrea coral puts on quite a display as the polyps extend to feed. Also at night you will encounter moray eels swimming freely about, an occasional lobster or octopus, and sponge crabs.

39

Klein Bonaire

Just-A-Nice-Dive 11

Typical depth range	:	15–100 feet
Typical current conditions	:	Light to moderate
Expertise required	:	Intermediate
Access	:	Boat

This site marks the eastern tip of Klein Bonaire. As the mooring is in 80–90 feet of water (although close to shore), this is best done as the first dive of the day. The reef starts close to shore and drops steeply down from 10–15 feet to 80–90 feet before reaching a sloping sand bottom. On the wall, there are large orange sponges, wire corals, leaf corals, and boulder corals ideally suited for wide-angle photography. Fish life is good, with tiger groupers, white-spotted filefish, Bermuda chubs, and, often seen, the Hawksbill turtle. There are French angelfish and yellowtail snappers as well. The area between this site and Ebo's reef offers some world-class wide-angle photo possibilities.

The black-and-white sea lily (Nemaster grandis) *normally rests, fully exposed, on sponges or coral outcroppings, with arms outstretched to catch plankton. (Photo: J. Schnabel)*

Typical depth range	:	15–100 feet
Typical current conditions	:	Light to moderate
Expertise required	:	Intermediate
Access	:	Boat

This site is one of the most recent diving additions to Klein Bonaire. Located on the southeast coast of Klein Bonaire, the mooring buoy is located in 25 feet of water amid lush soft corals. The soft corals mix with prolific mountainous star corals and other hard coral formations at the reef crest in 40 feet of water. The wall slope here is steep and covered with purple tube sponges, orange elephant ear sponges, and sheet corals in the deeper water. Mahogany snappers, goatfish, tiger groupers, and French and smallmouth grunts make a colorful addition to the upper reef slope. The wall face has spotted morays, queen angelfish, and porcupinefish populating the coral valleys of the deep. The shallow zone extends 50 yards from shore and makes a great place for exploration. Hawksbill turtles, trumpetfish, and parrotfish are common here, and with a little effort you can turn up a frogfish or two.

Usually hidden on sponges, the longlure frogfish's (Antennarius multiocellatus) *lumpy body shape makes it very hard to find. (Photo: S. Swygert)*

The gorgonians form a dense forest at many shallow reef sites. They offer shelter to many species of fish and invertebrates. Look on their branches for flamingo tongue snails and seahorses. (Photo: S. Swygert)

Typical depth range	:	20–80 feet
Typical current conditions	:	Light
Expertise required	:	Intermediate
Access	:	Boat

On the western portion of Klein Bonaire along the south coast, this spot is an excellent site for photography. A shallow, 12-feet-deep flat terrace of rock and coral heads mark the reef close to shore. This steps down to a terrace 25 feet deep, with thick gorgonians and hard coral formations with some large sea fans. This area has schools of mahogany snappers, schoolmasters, tiger groupers, and goatfish. The wall drops off abruptly to depths over 130 feet deep, and along the wall face there are some vertical portions with undercut ledges. Large orange sponges and long purple tube sponges make this an ideal portion of the reef for wide-angle photography. To the west of the mooring buoy, at a depth of 40 feet, is a large ship's anchor embedded in the coral.

The schooling behavior of fish is usually for protection or for cooperative hunting. Mahogany snappers (Lutjanus mahogoni) *stay along the bottom of the reef in small groups. (Photo: J. Schnabel)*

Typical depth range	:	20–130 feet
Typical current conditions	:	Light
Expertise required	:	Intermediate
Access	:	Boat

Forest takes its name from the forests of black coral found there. One of the most requested dive sites of repeat divers to Bonaire (and understandably so), Forest is not to be missed when you come to Bonaire. Located on the south coast, it is marked by the last buoy before rounding the southwest corner of Klein Bonaire. The shallow zone has elkhorn corals, large sea fans, and abundant gorgonians. The drop-off zone is a buttress of mountainous star coral with sea fans and soft corals in abundance. The wall starts in 40 feet of water and drops vertically, with a significant undercut ledge, just east of the mooring, which is covered with black coral, a huge orange elephant ear sponge, and lush gorgonians.

At a depth of 50 feet and deeper, many large, orange elephant ear sponges create incredible sites for wide-angle photography. Along the upper edge of the drop-off you will see scrawled filefish, mahogany snappers, white-spotted filefish, tiger groupers, and somewhat oversized porcupinefish, reaching 3 feet in length.

The uncommon marbled grouper (Epinephelus inermis) *is a valued sighting for fish watchers. (Photo: J. Schnabel)*

Southwest Corner 15

Typical depth range	: 25–120 feet
Typical current conditions	: Moderate to heavy
Expertise required	: Advanced
Access	: Boat

As its name implies, this site is located on the very southwestern corner of Klein Bonaire. As we have been teaching underwater photography on Bonaire for more than 5 years, first with Peter Hughes and now with our own company, Photo Tours, we have our favorite dive sites. The sites of southwest Klein Bonaire are, in our opinion, not to be surpassed anywhere in the world. From the shoreline to the bottom of the reef, the formations are incredible. Beginning in the shallows, the staghorn corals are thicker and higher than anywhere else, the soft corals stand taller than 6 feet, and the mountainous star coral formations are a towering 10 feet tall.

Large tiger and yellowmouth groupers enjoy cleaning stations under ledges of coral. There is a resident golden coney in the shallows, numerous scrawled and white-spotted filefish, and blue tangs in large schools that sweep the reef clean of algae. Queen angelfish are everywhere, as are French angelfish. The wall face begins in 40 feet of water and drops steeply down to a sandy bottom at 120 feet. The wall is alive with endless iridescent vase sponges, orange sponges, and green (as well as purple) tube sponges.

The rare golden coney (Cephalopholis fulvus) *has been a resident of Southwest Corner for years. Shy, yet curious, its favorite coral head is near the mooring. (Photo: J. Schnabel)*

Bonaire has long been noted for its excellent visibility, particularly here at Southwest Corner. (Photo: J. Schnabel)

Typical depth range	:	20–120 feet
Typical current conditions	:	Moderate to heavy
Expertise required	:	Advanced
Access	:	Boat

The next buoy north of Southwest Corner is named after Illinois dive-shop owner Elmer Munk, who has been bringing his dive groups to Bonaire for the past 10 years. Elmer fell in love with this portion of the Klein Bonaire reef and is honored by its name. The mooring buoy is in just 10 feet of water and is in an area of thick staghorn coral interspersed with heavy gorgonian growth. Large mountainous star coral formations rise up 10 feet from the bottom and are common all the way to the drop-off. The drop-off starts at 40 feet deep and slopes steeply down to 120 feet before ending in a sand bottom. As the current sometimes can be strong at these dive sites, be sure to begin your dive into the current.

Munk's Haven has perhaps more groupings of iridescent vase sponges than any other site on Bonaire, making this site an excellent place for wide-angle photography. Large, orange elephant ear sponges, mountainous star corals, and brain corals provide sheltering places for the many large tiger groupers to be found here. A 6-foot-long green moray eel also can often be found under one of the many dome-shaped star corals.

Iridescent azure vase sponge
*(*Callyspongia plicifera)
shown here with a black feather
crinoid. (Photo: J. Schnabel)

Sharon's Serenity*

Typical depth range   : 20–130 feet
Typical current conditions   : Moderate
Expertise required   : Intermediate
Access   : Boat

A relatively new dive site is located near the lighthouse on the south-western corner of Klein Bonaire. This is a good location for snorkelers as the mooring buoy is close to shore. There are numerous elkhorn and staghorn corals mixed with prolific soft corals in this shallow zone. The current, at times, can be a nuisance, but it is not as bad here as at Southwest Corner or Munk's Haven. The shallow coral shelf extends offshore 50 yards until the reef crests at 30 feet deep, with high-profile mountainous star coral formations becoming more obvious. As the drop-

The tiger grouper (Mycteroperca bonaci) *visits a cleaning station where small gobies remove parasites from its skin. (Photo: S. Swygert)*

As soon as a coral head topples, new corals spring up to cover the exposed portions. Competition for space on the reef in Bonaire is very keen for all the hard and soft corals. Sharon's Serenity. (Photo: J. Schnabel)

off plummets downward, dome-like formations of mountainous star coral protrude upwards, at 40 feet, creating a mushroom forest effect.

Among these protrusions, tiger groupers pull into cleaning stations to have pesky parasites removed by neon gobies and juvenile Spanish hogfish. There is a resident cubera snapper weighing in at over 100 pounds, and a jewfish of mammoth proportions has also been spotted here. Basket starfish are quite common on this side of Klein Bonaire. Therefore, night diving is highly recommended to view their nocturnal display. The wall is quite deep, and you need to watch your depth gauge carefully.

Typical depth range	:	20–120 feet
Typical current conditions	:	Light
Expertise required	:	Novice
Access:	:	Boat

Aggressor III is located at the second buoy south of the northwest corner of Klein Bonaire. A small native fishing hut is adjacent to the dive buoy, and when fishing activity takes place, it's not uncommon to see reef sharks swimming in for the leftovers. Don't be alarmed — they won't bother you, it's only the fish they are after.

The shallow zone here has thick growths of gorgonians, sea rods, and sea whips. A virtual soft coral forest is located on the upper reef slope and shallows and extends more than 60 yards from shore. Trumpetfish abound at this location, with the beautiful yellow trumpetfish standing out among the purple, brown, and silver ones. Close to the mooring, the drop-off opens into an arched shape, with two buttresses of coral mountains on each side.

The slope terraces down, with small sand ledges in 50–80 feet of water. Sand diver lizardfish and scorpionfish often hide in this area. Thick finger coral growth, plate corals, and mountainous star corals dominate the buttresses down to 80 feet, where wire corals become more pronounced. Web burrfish, white-spotted filefish, scrawled cowfish, and smooth trunkfish populate the upper shoulder of the drop-off. The coral crevices of the wall face provide niches for goldentail morays and spotted morays.

The squirrelfish (Holocentrus rufus) *displays its long dorsal spine when aroused. A nocturnal fish, it has large eyes for better nighttime vision. (Photo: J. Schnabel)*

Typical depth range	:	20–150 feet
Typical current conditions	:	Light to moderate
Expertise required	:	Intermediate
Access	:	Boat

Named after underwater photographer Carl Roessler, this is an exceptionally good dive for photography. The site is on the very northwest tip of Klein Bonaire. The drop-off begins only 20 yards from shore. The site is characterized by a sheer vertical wall of coral east of the buoy, beginning in 20 feet of water and dropping to 70 feet. It then slopes steeply to 150 feet deep before reaching a sandy bottom. In the shallows close to shore, good growths of elkhorn coral can be found, making this site pleasant for snorkeling.

Parrotfish, schools of blue tangs, and yellowtail snappers populate the shallow zone, with large tiger groupers sheltering along the drop-off. The vertical wall face is covered with tubastrea coral, tube sponges, and

Porpoises often swim close to shore along the coast of Klein Bonaire, sometimes sharing special moments with divers thrilled at their sight. Carl's Hill. *(Photo: J. Schnabel)*

The sheer vertical wall at Carl's Hill makes for great underwater photography. (Photo: J. Schnabel)

encrusting sponges. There are bristle worms on the wall face, providing for good macrophotography possibilities. Barracudas can often be seen in the blue water, along with bar jacks, and, occasionally, porpoises, which are seen swimming past this site on their way to southern waters. The wall face south of the buoy has numerous purple tube sponges. In the shallows, the soft corals become increasingly heavy as you approach Aggressor III.

Leonora's Reef* 20

Typical depth range	: 20–130 feet
Typical current conditions	: Light
Expertise required	: Novice
Access	: Boat

This site is oriented along the northwestern portion of Klein Bonaire, and is the first buoy east from Carl's Hill. The shallow zone of this region is typically overlaid with dense vertical stands of blade-like fire coral, brain corals, and low-profile mountainous star coral. Gorgonians are not as numerous here as they are at locations to the west. Adjacent to the mooring is a very large configuration of mountainous star coral along with black coral and several gorgonians in only 40 feet of water. There is a small tunnel through the structure, making an ideal frame for a picture of your buddy. This star coral is also undercut and encrusted with orange tubastrea coral.

The drop-off is steep and reaches depths greater than 130 feet. Plate coral is the dominant coral in the deep zone, with mountainous star coral in the intermediate depths. From the mooring east 50 yards is an exceptionally nice cluster of purple tube sponges in 40 feet of water, and east another 20 yards is a large growth of finger sponges in 80 feet of water. Both are good subjects for photography. Tiger groupers tend to predominate the deeper waters here, with parrotfish, yellowtail snappers, and four-eyed butterflyfish prevalent in the shallows. Close to the moorings are several tall columns of pillar coral, and lizardfish can be found in the sand patches nearby. West of the mooring in 20 feet of water is a large outcropping of mountainous star coral dependably sheltering a large school of goatfish and, occasionally, schoolmasters.

These giant purple tube sponges are typically found from depths of 40–80 feet deep, protruding from the coral wall face. Leonora's Reef. *(Photo: J. Schnabel)*

Typical depth range	: 20–130 feet
Typical current conditions	: Light
Expertise required	: Intermediate
Access	: Boat

Sampler is positioned on the north coast of Klein Bonaire and is the first buoy west of No Name Beach. The shallow section of reef is comprised of sandy areas in 10–20 feet of water with finger corals, isolated small brain corals, and mustard hill coral. There are a lot of parrotfish in the shallows and, upon entering the water, yellowtail snappers and friendly French angelfish will come to greet you.

Sampler is relatively low-profile, with a few nice tube sponge formations. The reef begins to fall off abruptly less than 20 yards from shore, and at a depth of 40 feet under the mooring there are several curious rock

Curious French angelfish (Pomacanthus paru) are very unafraid of divers and literally pose for photos. They gladly accept handouts; however, their normal diet consists of algae and sponges. (Photo: J. Schnabel)

Spotted moray eels
(Gymnothorax moringa) *are*
common on the reefs of
Bonaire. Daytime they are
curled beneath ledges of
coral and at night they swim
freely about the reef in search
of food. (Photo: J. Schnabel)

hinds. Sampler is distinguished from other sites on Bonaire in that it has been the location of extensive moray eel feeding. It was closed in March 1989 and reopened in March 1990, in order to give the reef a rest from being Bonaire's most popular dive site.

What makes this dive so special is that you don't have to swim far, because everything happens right under the boat. The multitudes of fish life that were attracted in the past still all look at you as though you are the one carrying the food. More tame fish will be seen at Sampler than at any other dive site in Bonaire.

Face-to-face with Moray Eels

Swimming along the reef face in 40 feet of water, spotted morays still swim up off of the reef to investigate divers for chunks of fish. One word of caution: keep your eyes towards the reef and stay alert. If an eel does annoy you, slowly ascend, as it will then swim back down to the reef. If morays are not your cup of tea, then do not dive here.

Typical depth range	:	40–120 feet
Typical current conditions	:	Light to moderate
Expertise required	:	Intermediate
Access	:	Boat

Rick Frehsee refers to an image that speaks for a particular destination as a "signature shot." For years, photojournalists have chosen Ebo's Reef as the place to make an image that sums up Bonaire in one picture. This can be attributed to the splendid display of giant orange elephant ear sponges, which are concentrated along the reef face in depths from 40–80 feet and topped with numerous black feather crinoids. These formations extend to the east and west more than a half tank of compressed air, and it is impossible to see them all.

Bonaire's most often used signature shot — a diver with orange sponge and crinoids — can be easily taken at beautiful Ebo's Reef. (Photo: J. Schnabel)

The queen angelfish (Holacanthus ciliaris) *is perhaps the most beautiful of all Caribbean tropical fish. Common in Bonaire, they frequent almost all the dive sites. (Photo: J. Schnabel)*

The best place to dive this site is under the mooring area and, as there is usually a current, your direction will be determined by the way it is moving. The mooring barrels are in 90 feet of water, so it is best to snorkel over to shore and begin your dive down the sand shoot opposite the buoy. Black coral is dense, as are feather crinoids, purple tube sponges, and wire corals. Creole wrasses can always be seen here swarming the reef in seemingly endless schools. Bermuda chubs, grey chromis, and friendly queen angelfish swim in and out along the drop-off.

North

Front Porch* 23

Typical depth range	: 15–80 feet
Typical current conditions	: Light to moderate
Expertise required	: Novice
Access	: Shore

Front Porch is located in front of the Sunset Beach Hotel, and access is convenient from either the dive pier or the beach. As this area is well protected, it makes a great site for snorkeling or SCUBA training dives. The drop-off under the dive pier begins in 15 feet of water and is marked by a sand slope with a large ship's anchor and an intact tugboat wreck at a depth of 50–75 feet. The tugboat is covered with bright orange tubastrea coral, fire coral, and Christmas tree worms. In this area, you will find a green moray eel that visits the wreck often, horse-eye jacks schooling around the wreck, and several large groupers. Proceed north, as the current is almost always coming from that direction. The sand extends some 70 feet north before a buttress of coral and sponges forms the reef system.

Front Porch is characterized by a steep wall that begins in 20 feet of water and reaches more than 100 feet deep before leveling off into sand. There are numerous purple tube sponges and good growths of mountainous star coral. Doubling back at 1,500 pounds of air, you should ascend up into the shallows where you may find a frogfish in the thick clusters of green finger sponges. Goatfish, parrotfish, and French angelfish seem to dominate this upper reef crest. Under the dive pier there are several scorpionfish blending into the rocks, so it is wise to watch out what you are touching in this area. The dive pier also shelters schools of grunts and goatfish. Night snorkeling and diving are highly recommended here.

The small tugboat "New York," located at Front Porch, has an interesting array of coral growth and marine life, including a resident green moray eel.
(Photo: J. Schnabel)

Typical depth range	:	20–120 feet
Typical current conditions	:	Light to moderate
Expertise required	:	Novice
Access	:	Shore

Bari is the house reef of the Sand Dollar Dive and Photo Complex, and is perfect for snorkeling and SCUBA training activities. There is a large diver service deck with plenty of trained instructors on hand to offer assistance. From the deck out to 100 yards there is a flat, sandy plateau, with isolated small brain corals, mustard hill corals, and gorgonians. The reef crest is from 20–40 feet deep and is covered primarily with mountainous star coral and soft corals. Sponges are numerous on the reef slope and there is a large barrel sponge at a depth of 130 feet, straight out from the dive deck.

There is usually a current here, so begin your dive into the current and when at 1,500 psi return via the shallow shoulder of the drop-off. The staff will be glad to advise you of the whereabouts of the resident frogfish, seahorses, and fingerprint cowries. Mullets can be seen in the shallow sand flats, as well as peacock flounders, scorpionfish, and goatfish. Outer reef fish are tiger groupers, French angelfish, and four-eyed butterflyfish. This site is a good night dive as there are usually large tarpons that prey upon the silver minnows visible in the beam of your dive light.

Silvery tarpons (Megalops atlantica) *often swim along the reef area in front of the Sand Dollar Beach Club. They feed on silver minnows and schools of scads, shown here at Bari Reef. (Photo J. Schnabel)*

Typical depth range	: 20–120 feet
Typical current conditions	: Light to moderate
Expertise required	: Novice
Access	: Shore

Named for the wreck of the *La Machaca*, a 45-foot native-built fishing vessel located 100 feet from shore in 45 feet of water and home of Mr. Rogers, an 8-foot-long green moray eel, La Machaca is the reef located in front of Capt'n Don's Habitat, and is excellent for snorkeling and diver training. Two large dive docks, "Papa Dock," for boat dives, and "Baby Dock," for shore dives, enclose a large diver platform with camera rinse, showers, and equipment storage.

A full staff of instructors is on hand if needed, and can advise you of the location of marine life and wrecks. The reef begins at shore with heavy elkhorn corals extending in a northward direction, making this a

This rather large red hind (Epinephelus guttatus) *relaxes while being cleaned by a sharknose* goby (Gobiosoma evelynae). *(Photo: J. Schnabel)*

The wreck of the La Machaca *rests in only 40 feet of water in front of Captain Don's Habitat.* La Machaca *is colorful and heavily encrusted with coral growth. (Photo: J. Schnabel)*

good snorkel trail. The shallow reef from 15 feet to 40 feet has lots of brain corals, mustard hill corals, and small tube sponge formations.

The reef slope is dotted with large domes of mountainous star coral, purple tube sponges, and orange elephant ear sponges. At a depth of 130 feet, there is a 55-foot fishing boat upright in the sand just to the north of "Baby Dock." As this is a relatively deep dive, you need to plan it carefully and include some safety decompression stops. The wreck is home to large schools of horse-eye jacks, tarpons, and groupers. To the south in 40 feet of water is "Reef 44 Scientifico," where a grid system had been constructed to monitor algae growth on the reef. Night diving on this reef is excellent as there are sleeping parrotfish and spotted moray eels swimming freely in search for food.

Typical depth range	:	20–70 feet
Typical current conditions	:	Light to moderate
Expertise required	:	Novice
Access	:	Shore or boat

Cliff is located in front of the Hamlet Villas north of Habitat. There is an easy sand beach entry adjacent to the dive buoy. A channel is marked through the dense elkhorn coral of the shallows, opening into a flat 50-foot-long shelf of low-profile hard and soft corals. The average depth of the shelf is 20 feet. The reef crests in only 30 feet of water and drops immediately to 70 feet deep with a sand ledge 5-feet-wide, before sloping off to 130 feet and a sandy bottom. This abrupt drop creates an exceptional miniwall, which is a splendid location for both macro and wide-angle photography.

The wall face is decorated with large orange sponges, tube sponges, and wire corals, with numerous bristle worms and anemones. The miniwall extends in both directions for some distance. If the current permits, swim to the south along the wall face, where you will find some cleaning stations that tiger groupers frequent. Return on the shoulder of the drop-off and you will see Capt'n Don's stone memorial to "divers who have gone before us," which is marked by an underwater dive flag.

The miniwall at Cliff is an excellent location for underwater photography. The wall drops steeply from 30–70 feet deep, providing shelter for intricate invertebrate life. (Photo: J. Schnabel)

Typical depth range	:	20–120 feet
Typical current conditions	:	Light to moderate
Expertise required	:	Novice
Access	:	Shore or boat

The mooring buoy for this site is opposite the Black Durgon Inn, and is a good reef for snorkelers as it is well protected. The mooring barrels rest in only 10 feet of water, elkhorn coral grows close to shore, and the shallow zone is populated by finger corals, brain corals, and gorgonians. There is an excellent miniwall that begins 100 feet from shore in 40 feet of water and drops vertically to 70 feet. As you proceed south, the wall formations become more dramatic, with a large cave arched out of the lower ledge in 60 feet of water. The cave is often a resting place for green moray eels or nurse sharks. Below the cave, large orange elephant

During the spring and summer months, schools of bigeye scads (Selar crumenophthalmus) *swarm over the reefs along the west coast of Bonaire.* Small Wall. (*Photo: J. Schnabel*)

The thick soft coral growth along the upper slope at Small Wall has, for years, made this a good location for finding seahorses. (Photo: J. Schnabel)

ear sponges are prolific, making this a good location for wide-angle photography.

The upper reef crest is a maze of soft corals and small finger sponges, where seahorses, with their tails typically curled around the branches of these structures, can be found. Yellowtail snappers and French angelfish entertain divers in their pursuit of handouts. Night dives are good here, frequently turning up a spiny Caribbean lobster.

Typical depth range	:	20–120 feet
Typical current conditions	:	Light
Expertise required	:	Novice
Access	:	Shore or boat

These two sites are located at the first buoys north after passing the desalination plant. A dirt road off of the main road provides access to a small rocky beach. Since they are almost identical in profile we shall discuss both sites as one.

Moored in 15 feet of water, with ample staghorn, finger, and fire corals in the shallows, both sites show little diver impact as they are new as of 1989. In 20–40 feet of water there are parrotfishes grazing on abundant hard coral sculptures, with numerous anemones and tall soft coral gorgonians sheltering trumpetfish. Upon close examination, the gorgonians and sea rods provide a safe haven to slender filefish. The Andrea sections of reef are popular with local divemasters, as they almost always locate seahorses here.

The reef crests in 50 feet of water, with tall gorgonians and substantial mountainous star coral growth. The wall is a series of winding undersea canyons dropping down to a sandy bottom in 80 feet of water. Tube sponges, sheet corals, and wire corals decorate the lower wall face. Lobsters and large spider crabs inhabit the spaces between the sheet corals. Red-and-white banded coral shrimps and glasseye snappers tend to seek refuge in the mountainous star coral crevices of the upper wall slope.

Giant Caribbean anemones (Condylactic gigantea) *are predators that feed on plankton and small fishes.* (Photo: J. Schnabel)

65

Typical depth range	:	20–130 feet
Typical current conditions	:	Light
Expertise required	:	Novice
Access	:	Shore or boat

Weber's Joy was opened in March 1990 to boat diving, with a buoy placed adjacent to an abandoned small house along the coastal road north. This site has been referred to as "Witch's Hut" by photographers for years, and is an easy roadside entry over smooth, broken coral stones.

The shallow zone has good elkhorn coral growth, with lots of pretty tropicals making it good for snorkelers. This shelf extends outward some 100 feet to 30 feet of water and is marked by staghorn coral, finger coral, and brain corals. Angelfish, rock beauties, and butterflyfish are predomin-

Honeycomb cowfish (Lactophrys polygonia) *can be found at almost every dive site. Be careful of the crenelated fire coral* (Millepora alcicornis). *It is very common in the shallows and causes painful welts when touched. (Photo: J. Schnabel)*

The yellowmouth grouper (Mycteroperca interstitialis) *is one of the many types of groupers that can be found on Bonaire. (Photo: J. Schnabel)*

ant here. Both east and west directions are similar, so the current will be your guide as to which direction you take.

The drop-off at 40 feet deep is defined by tall stands of gorgonians and sea whips positioned around high reliefs of mountainous star corals. These formations are undercut and encrusted with tubastrea coral, which form cleaning stations visited by yellowmouth and tiger groupers. The wall slopes off steeply down to 130 feet before leveling to a sand bottom. The wall face is alive with purple tube sponges, orange sponges, and finger sponges. As there are high reliefs of mountainous star coral and abundant fish life, this site is popular among underwater photographers.

Typical depth range	:	20–130 feet
Typical current conditions	:	Light
Expertise required	:	Novice
Access	:	Shore or boat

This is an easy site to find as it is next to the Radio Netherlands towers, with an overlook and convenient parking. There are about 64 steps down to the water; however, it feels like 1,000 on the way back up with SCUBA gear. To dive here, you should be in good enough shape to carry your gear back up the steps or, better yet, try it from a boat.

This site has perhaps the largest protective cove of any other, providing a shallow shelf that is covered with staghorn coral, brain coral, mustard hill coral, and gorgonians. Hawksbill turtles can often be seen in this area. The mooring buoy is close to the drop-off in 20 feet of water, and

The distinctive yellow and purple Spanish hogfish (Bodianus rufus) *can be found swimming about the reef at 1,000 Steps. (Photo: S. Swygert)*

*An approaching manta ray (*Manta birostris)*, often seen in the vicinity of 1,000 Steps. Mantas filter-feed on plankton in the water and swim in the open ocean, sometimes passing over reef areas. (Photo: J. Schnabel)*

is surrounded by extremely high-profile mountainous star corals, some towering more than 12 feet tall. These types of formations extend both west as far as you can swim on a half tank of air, and to the east for 50 yards or more.

The preferred direction from the mooring is to the west if the current permits. There are numerous schools of mahogany snappers, schoolmasters, and goatfish here. Blue tangs often swim in large numbers to clean the reef of algae. The drop-off is a mixture of hard corals with a few purple tube sponges, and is not as interesting as the shallow zone, which is alive with fish activity.

However, keep an eye open to the blue water at the drop-off. Anything can happen here, as this site has provided glimpses of manta rays, whale sharks, and other large pelagics. Dolphins often pass by here and pilot whales sometimes appear in the winter months.

Typical depth range	: 20–130 feet
Typical current conditions	: Light to moderate
Expertise required	: Novice to intermediate
Access	: Boat

Etched out of the ironshore and the first buoy north of 1,000 Steps, Bon Bini Na Cas ("welcome to my home" in Papiamento, the native language of Bonaire) is an excellent addition to the magnificent northern dive sites. The buoy lies in the center of a small cove, providing just enough sea room between the buoy and the vertical cliff face to position a dive boat. The shallow shelf has a large area of sand mixed with soft corals and sea fans. Hard corals and sponges are denser towards the drop-off in 40 feet of water.

Creole wrasses, blue tangs, trumpetfish, and French angelfish are active in the shallows and the upper reef slope. Along the wall face in 60–80 feet of water, iridescent vase sponges, along with yellow and purple tube sponges, protrude, providing good photo opportunities. There are several large clusters of finger sponges in both directions from the mooring, found in depths from 50–80 feet. Trumpetfish and tiger groupers can often be found sheltering amid these sponges.

The sloping wall at Bon Bini Na Cas is alive with many different sponge formations. This new dive site is proving to be much in demand. (Photo: J. Schnabel)

Ol' Blue* 32

Typical depth range	: 20–130 feet
Typical current conditions	: Light to moderate
Expertise required	: Novice to intermediate
Access	: Shore or boat

Ol' Blue is the long coral beach east of 1,000 Steps, and entry is provided over broken coral stones. You will definitely need dive booties to protect your feet if diving from shore. There is a large protected cove with a shallow shelf in 20 feet of water, which extends seaward 100 yards.

The dive mooring buoy is just east of the beach entry zone and is

Ol' Blue has an abundance of queen angelfish. This one follows divers on their dive, and is aptly nicknamed Ol' Blue. (Photo: J. Schnabel)

Invertebrate life in Bonaire is always full of surprises. This rarely seen calico crab (Hepatus epheliticus) *sits atop a soft coral branch at Ol' Blue. (Photo: S. Swygert)*

positioned in 15 feet of water. The shallow plateau is prolific with staghorn coral, sea fans, and soft corals. There are numerous friendly French angelfish, and one queen angelfish that follows divers everywhere. The reef crests in only 25 feet of water and is characterized by mountainous star corals, gorgonians, and various other hard coral formations.

The wall face is a mixture of finger corals in the shallows, boulder coral, and mountainous star coral in 40–70 feet of water, with sheet corals and wire corals extending down to 150 feet, where the slope finally levels off into sand. Numerous large boulders have fallen off into the water on the eastern end of the cove creating a series of high-profile fish shelters. Horse-eye jacks are common in this area with some tiger groupers and mahogany snappers. Ol' Blue is definitely a dive not to be missed, and an old favorite of repeat divers to Bonaire.

Typical depth range	:	25–130 feet
Typical current conditions	:	Light to moderate
Expertise required	:	Intermediate
Access	:	Boat

Rappel is the most often requested dive site by repeat visitors to Bonaire. Perhaps this is due to the fact that it is unlike any other site on Bonaire. Named Rappel because you would have to rappel down a cliff face to get there from shore, the mooring is in 30 feet of water on a ledge that is about 100 feet wide, extending out from a vertical cliff rising 60 feet above the water's surface.

The sheer cliff face underwater is covered with thick growths of sea fans and soft corals. The shallow ledge is covered with huge sea fans, brain corals, and mountainous star corals, all of which take on larger proportions than at most other sites. The waterline is undercut in some places and white water from crashing waves above can be viewed from underwater, providing unique photo opportunities.

Eighty yards south of the mooring, there is a large cave sheltering a resident oversized black grouper and several tiger groupers awaiting their turn to visit the cave. The wall below the mooring is a large precipice of mountainous star corals, and a sand ledge is etched out of this formation at 80 feet deep. Wire corals extend out from the precipice, and tubastrea coral grows on the underside of the ledges. Below 80 feet deep, dense blankets of sheet coral cover the wall face to depths below 130 feet. The upper ledge makes a good place for ending your dive and searching for nudibranchs. There are more varieties in abundance here than at any of the other sites.

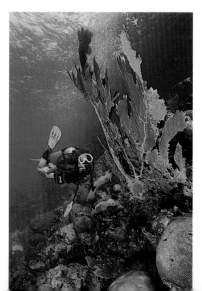

Common sea fan (Gorgonia ventalina) *found along the colorful and distinctive cliff of Rappel. The waves can be seen crashing overhead. (Photo: J. Schnabel)*

73

Typical depth range	:	15–130 feet
Typical current conditions	:	Light
Expertise required	:	Intermediate
Access	:	Boat

Years ago, Captain Don Stewart led leap dives to Karpata. This required leaping into the water at La Dania's and drifting to Karpata. Hence, the name La Dania's Leap. Today, we don't recommend doing this unless Captain Don leads the way, as once you have entered, the only way out is Karpata.

The mooring is in 15 feet of water and is surrounded by elkhorn coral. There is a narrow ledge of sea fans and soft corals before the wall drops off immediately. La Dania's wall is one of Bonaire's truly vertical walls, with awesome canyons and sand shoots. Large orange sponges and tube sponges protrude through the thick coral covering of the wall. Wire corals are extremely heavy in 80 feet of water on the lower portion of the drop-off.

The canyons wind in and out going both north and south, creating spectacular vistas when viewed from below looking up. Tiger groupers seek cleaning stations along the wall face, and black corals grow as shallow as 40 feet in some places. The shallow shoulder of the drop-off has many trumpetfishes, parrotfishes, and white-spotted filefishes.

The banded butterflyfish (Chaetodon striatus) *can often be found swimming in the shallow waters of Bonaire. (Photo: J. Schnabel)*

The wall at La Dania's Leap is covered by wire coral. This is one of the most vertical walls in Bonaire, making for excellent photo opportunities. (Photo: J. Schnabel)

Typical depth range	:	25–130 feet
Typical current conditions	:	Light to moderate
Expertise required	:	Novice to intermediate
Access	:	Shore or boat

Karpata is well-known to old salts familiar with Bonaire, and a favorite location among visitors. A large yellow stone bearing the dive site's name marks the shore entrance along the northern coastal road. Karpata is the location of the Netherlands Antilles National Parks Foundation (STINAPA). Here, Dutch scientists and students study the coral reef ecology of the Netherlands Antilles.

Shore entry is down a short cement stairway to a small dock. Waves sometimes break over outlying elkhorn coral, and there is a small channel 5 feet wide by 20 feet long etched out of the coral, through which you swim out to the reef. Just 50 feet from shore, the reef steps down from

One of the many large ships' anchors to be found at Karpata, shown here in less than 40 feet of water. (Photo: J. Schnabel)

Stoplight parrotfish (Sparisoma viride) *are found in abundance on Bonaire and are studied at the Karpata Ecological Center. Their sharp teeth and powerful jaws enable them to eat hard corals. (Photo: J. Schnabel)*

10 to 20 feet deep, opening into a valley characterized by large sea fans, purple tube sponges, and ample soft corals. The bottom takes a steep, almost vertical drop to more than 130 feet deep. Exploring the wall face to the south leads to several large anchors; one lays embedded at about 35 feet and is a great subject for wide-angle photography.

Visibility at Karpata is sometimes 200 feet and the wall is a series of magnificent coral canyons with large orange sponge formations. Return to the shoulder of the drop-off when you reach 1,500 psi and enjoy the numerous soft corals and fans. French angelfish, parrotfish, trumpetfish, and barracudas are in abundance here.

Washington Park

Typical depth range	:	25–130 feet
Typical current conditions	:	Moderate to heavy
Expertise required	:	Intermediate to advanced
Access	:	Boat

Located just south of Boca Slagbaai, the mooring marking this site is located in 30 feet of water. This dive site consists of a broad, shallow shelf extending 150 feet from shore with an average depth of 30 feet. The reef then crests in 40 feet of water and the drop-off begins abruptly, plummeting vertically down to 130 feet.

The current usually runs north to south, so you will be swimming north through corals of mammoth proportions. The shallow shelf has some of

A diver enjoys the bright color of the orange sponge. (Photo: J. Schnabel)

A crinoid is found on a deepwater gorgonian (Iciligorgia schrammi), which is surrounded by orange sponge, a typical example of the scenic array of shapes and hues so often found in clusters on Bonaire. (Photo: S. Swygert)

the largest corals to be seen anywhere — brain corals over 6 feet in diameter, soft corals 8 feet tall, and mountainous star coral domes 15 feet tall. Barracudas, viper morays, schoolmasters, coneys, and scrawled filefish are native to the upper reef. Along the face of the drop-off, large mountains of coral shelter green morays under their ledges.

Creole wrasses engulf the upper wall slope. At times their schools extend to the limits of visibility in both directions. Schools of horse-eye jacks soar in the blue water offshore, and whale sharks have been sighted here in winter months. Close to shore, there are large boulders fallen from the ironshore centuries ago, now covered with sea fans and soft corals. Turtles often glide through this region.

Typical depth range	:	15–130 feet
Typical current conditions	:	Moderate
Expertise required	:	Intermediate
Access	:	Shore or boat

An ideal location for a beach outing, snorkelers and children will enjoy the large sand and coral beach entry zone. The sand continues into the sea and forms a large protected cove with an average depth of 25 feet. Coral heads close to shore harbor a myriad of tropicals. There are cannons in 10 feet of water just on the southern end of the cove. Palmetto fish school here in force, and iguanas watch from ironshore perches. The bay is alive with activity.

For SCUBA divers, begin your dive south along the coast in the shallow water. Impressive sea fans, soft corals, and acres of staghorn coral layer the shallow plateau. Turn out to the drop-off, which starts at 40 feet and is quite steep, and work your way back to Slagbaai along the wall face ascending to shallow water as you go. Horse-eye jacks, tiger groupers, and schoolmasters can be seen along the upper area of the drop-off. When you reach a sand valley, it's time to head back to shore. The sand will be on your left and coral on your right side. Sometimes this tack turns up a hawksbill turtle or moray eel and barracudas.

Bonaire offers divers and snorkelers an opportunity to observe and interact with marine life. A diver is shown hitching a ride on a hawksbill turtle. (Photo: J. Schnabel)

Typical depth range	:	15–130 feet
Typical current conditions	:	Moderate to heavy
Expertise required	:	Advanced
Access	:	Shore

A large, rocky sand beach opening into a cove filled with elkhorn and staghorn corals provides some of the best snorkeling close to shore that Bonaire has to offer. There is a break in the reef on the south side of the beach through which to enter. Begin working your way into the current immediately. This usually takes you north through a garden of staghorn, mountainous star coral, and leafy fire corals.

The shallow shelf continues a considerable distance to the drop-off (135 yards) across a bed of sand and staghorn corals. The wall face is fairly flat with some sponge formations and black coral, and there is usually a strong current. Along the wall, bar jacks and horse-eye jacks can be seen passing by in the blue water, while creole wrasses swim close to the reef. Plan your dive carefully, saving enough air for a lengthy swim back to shore. Midnight parrotfishes are common here, and you may encounter southern stingrays in the sand flats.

Club finger coral (Porites porites) *is native to the dive sites in the north. Many small invertebrates can be found hiding between the fingers.* Playa Funchi. *(Photo: J. Schnabel)*

Typical depth range	:	15–130 feet
Typical current conditions	:	Moderate to heavy
Expertise required	:	Advanced
Access	:	Shore

North of Playa Funchi along the northwest coast of the park, there is a small rocky beach entry that leads to a classic spur-and-groove network of coral spurs extending out from shore with sand grooves in between. These types of formations can only be seen here and at Boca Bartol. They are quite a change from the normal shallow reef of Bonaire. The northern route is the best dive at Benge, offering overall healthier corals. Large sea fans, mountainous star corals, staghorn coral, and blade fire coral are common in the shallow zone.

The swim out to the drop-off is more than 100 yards, with the water reaching 40 feet deep at the crest of the reef. At the point where the spurs break up, there are often large tiger groupers and southern stingrays in the area near the reef crest. The northern wall dive is very good, with abundant deep-water gorgonians and impressive sponge formations making it ideal for wide-angle photography. Plan your dive carefully if intending to visit the drop-off, as air consumption becomes an important factor.

A diver feels small swimming amongst the huge formations of mountainous star coral (Montastraea annularis) *at Playa Benge. (Photo: J. Schnabel)* ▶

Typical depth range	:	15–130 feet
Typical current conditions	:	Moderate to heavy
Expertise required	:	Advanced
Access	:	Shore

Boca Bartol is the northernmost dive site on Bonaire and is accessible by way of the park coastal road. Due to the close proximity of the windward side of the ocean, large swells sometimes roll into the cove at Bartol. Therefore, only dive here when the sea is very calm.

The entry zone is on the south end of the cove and is a difficult walk over slippery rocks, requiring good communication with your dive buddy. The site is a spur-and-groove complex unmatched in Bonaire, with large elkhorn corals, sea fans, and mountainous star corals creating a maze. The top of the coral spurs reach up to the surface in some places, and the sand valleys in between average 20 feet deep. From shore to the drop-off is a long 150-yard swim and not recommended, as there is plenty to see in the shallow water, including midnight parrotfish, black durgon, tiger groupers, and ocean triggerfish.

The spur-and-groove system ends in a large lake of sand where southern stingrays are common. You will need a compass to navigate across the sand flat to the sloping drop-off. This swim will take you out of sight of both the shallow and the deep reef for a short period of time. Two sand shoots pour down the slope, leaving a coral- and gorgonian-covered center island down to 80 feet, where the sand continues down deeper than 130 feet. Southern stingrays also can be found in the sand of the drop-off. Pelagics include horse-eye jacks, bar jacks, and an occasional eagle ray.

Common sea fans are picturesque as they gently sway with the current and surge. Boca Bartol. *(Photo: J. Schnabel)* ▶

3

Marine Life of Bonaire

Bonaire and Klein Bonaire are completely encircled by a fringing reef system, which is protected from spearfishing, divers sitting or standing on the coral, boats anchoring on the reefs, and the collection of coral. Nothing may be taken from the water, either dead or alive. This sort of protection of the reefs has brought about a very unique relationship between divers and the marine life of Bonaire. Nowhere else in the Caribbean are the fish so friendly or so unafraid. They have grown up to trust the diver, and do not fear pursuit or ending up on the tip of a spear pole. This friendliness has made it possible to study the behavior of the marine life from a close perspective.

Bonaire is the tip of a deep undersea mountain resulting from volcanic eruptions occurring more than 70 million years ago. The reef begins at the surface and descends to 200 feet, the depth of the Bonaire Marine Park. The shallow shelf surrounding Bonaire crests in an average of 20–40 feet. This fosters the growth of an extremely healthy reef ecosystem just offshore. There is intense competition for space between hard and soft corals, and these dense reefs of Bonaire are the underlying framework that host the most prolific populations of sponges, invertebrates, and fish in the Caribbean. Every available ecological niche is inhabited by marine life.

Sand patches are crowded in amongst thick coral growths in the shallow plateau areas, and scorpionfish, lizardfish, and peacock flounders are common. As soft corals are in abundance, so are flamingo tongue shells and fingerprint cowries, which prey upon the gorgonians, and camouflaged trumpetfish. The trumpetfish hang vertically until quickly darting down to engulf prey — more often than not a damselfish. More than 12 species of damselfish are commonly seen, and the territorial types often unexpectedly nip divers.

The hard corals become increasingly dense as the drop-off is approached, with large formations of mountainous star coral, finger corals, and brain corals. The crevices provide shelter for many species of moray eels, squirrelfish, and blackbar soldierfish. Under coral ledges, there are large concentrations of banded coral shrimps and arrowhead crabs staffing

Spotted cleaning shrimp (Periclimenes yucatanicus) can often be found with anemones. They clean debris and microorganisms off of fish. The shrimp will even clean a diver's fingernail if approached. (Photo: S. Swygert)

cleaning stations for fish and eels. Numerous sea anemones nestle in the reef and are home to cleaning shrimps and juvenile wrasses. Anemone shrimps and spotted cleaning shrimps maintain a mysterious symbiotic relationship with the anemones. They are immune to the sting of the anemone and attract small fish to the anemone, which they clean and the anemone often consumes. Nudibranchs are in abundance due to the high concentration of fire and staghorn corals. They lodge on the dead areas of each to feed on the algae growing there.

The keen competition for space on the reefs of Bonaire forces the corals and marine life to quickly establish territories in order to survive. Tube, vase, and encrusting sponges cement themselves to any dead coral skeleton. Sponges are the usual hiding spot for the frogfish, and their lumpy bodies are well camouflaged. The frogfish dangles a lure on a fishing-pole filament, which it waves about over its mouth to attract small fish. The fish approach and the frogfish leaps on its webbed pectoral fins and engulfs its prey — a fish that fishes for other fish! Sponges also shelter brittle starfish, juvenile fish, and cleaning gobies.

This longlure frogfish (Antennarius multiocellatus) *looks like a bright yellow sponge growing from the orange sponge. Note the extended lure. (Photo: J. Schnabel)*

Seahorses Are a Common Sight

Seahorses are plentiful in Bonaire, with ample soft corals providing necessary perches and protection. Seahorses are able to change their body color to a great degree and are sometimes hard to find as they blend in perfectly with their chosen habitat. Bright yellow, orange, pink, brown, and black are colors to try and spot; a mature seahorse can be as large as 6 inches long. The male seahorse has a brood pouch over its abdomen and the female seahorse goes from male to male laying eggs in the pouch. The male fertilizes them and gives live birth to baby seahorses.

Seahorses are unique in the fish world. Their tails do not have fins and they rarely swim great distances. Rather, they slowly glide along the bottom, and use their tail to hold fast to the coral. The transparent dorsal fin on the back beats up to 60 times per second! To a diver, a seahorse is a small, magical creature and entirely vulnerable. We ask that you handle these delicate animals without your gloves or, better yet, just look and don't touch.

These are some of the marine creatures of Bonaire that continue to fascinate visiting divers and scientists. Although large pelagics are not common, a manta ray did seek the help of divers to cut loose an entanglement of line and bottles. It's rare to see sharks on the leeward side of Bonaire, yet when a local fisherman regularly cleaned his fish on Klein Bonaire, black-tip sharks appeared almost immediately, swimming with divers for five months, until the fisherman stopped fishing that area. Porpoises can be seen many mornings in Boca Slagbaai and from there, swim to Klein Bonaire and south around the corner of the island. The north to south pattern almost always yields wonderful encounters between playful porpoises and dive boats. In the winter months, pilot whale and whale shark sightings are not uncommon.

There are many puzzles to the sea that remain unanswered, but Bonaire is a good place to study nature and enjoy the marine life living there. Bonaire's conservation measures and the careful diving practice of concerned divers will ensure the continued growth and health of Bonaire's lush reefs and marine life.

Pilot whales migrate through the waters of Bonaire. (Photo: J. Schnabel)

4

Safety

If you are diving with one of the hotels or dive operators on Bonaire, your safety will be of utmost importance to their divemasters and instructors. Dive profiles will be recommended and repetitive dive plans made to allow sufficient surface interval between dives. Your skill level will be noted and courses recommended to upgrade your certification if you so desire. You will not be, however, taken on guided dives and forced to follow a speedy divemaster around the reef and back to the boat in 10 minutes. Quite the opposite, divers are treated as adults, responsible for their own actions. You will make your own dive plan within the safe limits of sport diving, and plan your own repetitive dives, as many as you can safely do in one day.

This type of diving freedom requires the careful use of the dive tables or dive computers, and following good judgment in your diving practices. The divemasters of Bonaire have developed some techniques that will be suggested in your dive briefing and which are worth mentioning here. Your first dive of the day should be your deepest dive of the day — not more than 100 feet when diving with responsible operators. There is not much to see deeper than 100 feet in Bonaire anyway, so why push it? Begin your dive into the current so you may return to the boat with the current, decreasing air consumption. Turn around when you reach 1,500 psi and ascend to the shoulder of the drop-off (30 feet deep). Work your way back to your point of entry at this depth or shallower. This time spent with the second half of your air supply in shallow water has made for an incredible safety record in Bonaire. For, as you enjoy the dive on your return, you are slowly giving off excess nitrogen taken on during the deep portion of the dive. Make a safety stop at 10 feet for a few minutes after every dive. This helps eliminate nitrogen before surfacing even further. The worst thing any diver can do is to ascend directly to the surface from depth. A slow, gradual ascent is much safer.

Safe divers also practice certain unwritten rules when on a diving vacation. The word "vacation" suggests drinking, partying, staying up late — practices that are certainly fun, but ones which are not in your best interests on a diving vacation. Dive boats leave early in the morning.

Whenever traveling to a new diving destination, seek out the help and advice of local dive-masters about currents, weather, and dive site selection. Take additional instruction to sharpen your diving skills. (Photo J. Schnabel)

Staying up late and drinking all night will predispose you to the bends. Alcohol and drugs do not mix with safe diving practices. Get plenty of sleep, stay well-hydrated with water, and if you don't feel good, *don't dive*.

Bonaire Recompression Facility: There is a modern multiplace chamber facility at the San Francisco Hospital in downtown Kralendijk, Bonaire. A trained staff under the direction of resident diving physician Dr. Richard van der Vaart is on 24-hour call in the event of diving emergencies. The Police Emergency number is 8000, and the Hospital/Chamber number is 8900.

DAN: The Divers Alert Network (DAN), a membership association of individuals and organizations sharing a common interest in diving safety operates a **24-hour national hotline, (919) 684-8111** (collect calls are accepted in an emergency). DAN does not directly provide medical care; however, they do provide advice on early treatment, evacuation, and hyperbaric treatment of diving-related injuries. Additionally, DAN provides diving safety information to members to help prevent accidents.

Divers must be careful not to touch or come in contact with fire coral (Millepora alcicornis), *which is found in the shallow waters of Bonaire. It may cause painful welts and skin irritations. (Photo: J. Schnabel)*

Membership is $10 a year, offering: the DAN Underwater Diving Accident Manual, describing symptoms and first aid for the major diving related injuries; emergency room physician guidelines for drugs and i.v. fluids; a membership card listing diving-related symptoms on one side and DAN's emergency and non-emergency phone numbers on the other; 1 tank decal and 3 small equipment decals with DAN's logo and emergency number; and a newsletter, "Alert Diver," which describes diving medicine and safety information in layman's language, with articles for professionals, case histories, and questions related to diving. Special memberships for dive stores, dive clubs, and corporations are also available. The DAN Manual can be purchased for $4 from the Administrative Coordinator, National Diving Alert Network, Duke University Medical Center, Box 3823, Durham, NC 27710.

DAN divides the U.S. into 7 regions, each coordinated by a specialist in diving medicine who has access to the skilled hyperbaric chambers in his region. Non-emergency or information calls are connected to the DAN office and information number, (919) 684-2948. This number can be dialed direct, Monday–Friday between 9 a.m. and 5 p.m. Eastern Standard time. Divers should not call DAN for general information on chamber locations. Chamber status changes frequently making this kind of information dangerous if obsolete at the time of an emergency. Instead, divers should contact DAN as soon as a diving emergency is suspected to confirm the location of the nearest chamber. All divers should have comprehensive medical insurance and check to make sure that hyperbaric treatment and air ambulance are covered internationally. Luckily, Bonaire has a fully-staffed and equipped chamber. In the event of an accident, proceed to the San Francisco Hospital at once.

Diving is a safe sport and there are very few accidents compared to the number of divers and number of dives made each year. But when the infrequent injury does occur, DAN is ready to help. DAN, originally 100% federally funded, is now largely supported by the diving public. Membership in DAN or purchase of DAN manuals or decals provides divers with useful safety information and provides DAN with necessary operating funds. Donations to DAN are tax deductible, as DAN is a legal non-profit public service organization.

Though bristle worms (Hermodice carunculata) *are pretty and colorful to look at and photograph, they are dangerous to touch. The bristles can penetrate the skin and cause severe pain for several hours. (Photo: J. Schnabel)*

Appendix: Bonaire Dive Services

The list below is included as a service to the reader. The authors have made every effort to make this list complete at the time the book was printed. This list does not constitute an endorsement of these operators and dive shops.

Hotels with Diving and Photo Operations on Site

Captains Don's Habitat
1080 Port Boulevard, Suite 100
Miami, FL 33132
(800) 327-6709; fax (305) 371-2337
Bonaire: (599) 7-8290, fax: -8240

DIVI Flamingo Beach Resort
6340 Quadrangle Drive, Suite 300
Chapel Hill, North Carolina
27514-8900
(800) 367-3484; fax (919) 419-2075
Bonaire: (599) 7-8285, fax: -8238

Sand Dollar Condominium Resort
P. O. Box 3253
Longwood, Florida 32779
(800) 288-4773; fax: (407) 774-9322
Bonaire: (599) 7-8738, fax: -8760

Hotels with Diving on Site

Buddy Dive Resort
Kaya Gob. N. Debrot #85
Bonaire, Netherlands Antilles
Bonaire: (599) 7-5080; fax: -8647

Coral Regency Resort
Kaya Gob. N. Debrot #90
Bonaire, Netherlands Antilles
Bonaire: (599) 7-5580; fax: -5680

Harbor Village Beach Resort
Kaya Gob. N. Debrot #71
Bonaire, Netherlands Antilles

(800) 424-0004; fax: (305) 567-9659
Bonaire: (599) 7-7500; fax: -7507

Plaza Resort Bonaire
343 Neponset Street
Canton, Massachusetts 02021
(800) 766-6016; fax: (617) 821-1568
Bonaire: (599) 7-2500; fax: -7133

Sunset Beach Hotel
P.O. Box 333
Bonaire, Netherlands Antilles
(800) 344-4439
Bonaire: (599) 7-8448; fax: -8118

Guest Houses and Inns with Diving on Site

Black Durgon Inn/Bonaire Scuba Center
Kaya Gob. N. Debrot #145
Bonaire, Netherlands Antilles
(800) 526-2370
Bonaire: (599) 7-5736; fax: -8846

Carib Inn
P. O. Box 68
Bonaire, Netherlands Antilles
Bonaire: (599) 7-8819; fax: -5295
E-mail: 75317,667@Compuserve.
Com

Sunset Resorts–Villas & Apartments
P. O. Box 333
Bonaire, Netherlands Antilles
Bonaire: (599) 7-8448; fax: -8118

Independent Dive Operations

Blue Divers
Kaya den Tera #2
Bonaire, Netherlands Antilles
(599) 7-6860; fax: -6865

Dive Inn
P. O. Box 362
Bonaire, Netherlands Antilles
(599) 7-8761; fax: -8513

Patrick's Divers
Kaya Swesia #23
Bonaire, Netherlands Antilles
tel/fax: (599) 7-4080

Touch the Sea with Dee Scarr
P. O. Box 369
Bonaire, Netherlands Antilles
tel/fax: (599) 7-8529

Underwater Photo Operations

Photo Tours, NV
Kaya Gob. N. Debrot #129
Bonaire, Netherlands Antilles
(599) 7-5390; fax: -8060
E-mail: Jerry Schna@AOL.COM

Watercolours, NV
Kaya Kuarta #9
Bonaire, Netherlands Antilles
tel/fax: (599) 7-4089

Don't mistake the spotted scorpionfish (Scorpaena plumieri) for a rock on the reef. They camouflage themselves very well and when their spines are touched, the sting causes toxic infection and pain. (Photo: J. Schnabel)

Index

* Boldface numbers indicate photos.